Contents

Quick Man Tan

Everybody called him 'Quick Man Tan' when he was a young man. That was a long time ago. Now people called him by his real name – Caleb Tan.

Caleb liked to talk about the old days. He talked to anybody who was interested. He told them that when he was younger he could catch a fly in his hand.

That was how quick he was. Sometimes tourists came to his café for coffee or maybe some chicken with rice. When they had a meal was best. Then Caleb had more time to tell them how quick he once was. 'I was the best,' he told them. And, just to show them, he moved his hands in the air. He moved like the fighters in *kung fu* films.

80 002 823 734

Level 2

Series editor: Philip Prowse

Circle Games

Frank Brennan

CAMBRIDGE
UNIVERSITY PRESS

CAMBRIDGE UNIVERSITY PRESS
Cambridge, New York, Melbourne, Madrid, Cape Town, Singapore, São Paulo

Cambridge University Press
The Edinburgh Building, Cambridge CB2 2RU, UK

www.cambridge.org
Information on this title: www.cambridge.org/9780521630702

First published 2005
3rd printing 2006

Printed in the United Kingdom at the University Press, Cambridge

Illustrations by Paul McCaffrey (c/o Sylvie Poggio Agency)

A catalogue record for this publication is available from the British Library

ISBN-13 978-0-521-63070-2 paperback
ISBN-10 0-521-63070-3 paperback

ISBN-13 978-0-521-68609-9 paperback plus audio CD pack
ISBN-10 0-521-68609-1 paperback plus audio CD pack

'Nobody could fight like me,' he always said. 'I was the best in Singapore.' But he wasn't very quick now. He still knew what to do, but he was slower.

Usually, people smiled at him and finished their chicken with rice. But sometimes someone told Caleb he was a stupid old man. At those times he went back into the kitchen and May May, his wife, talked to them. 'Please don't mind my husband,' she laughed to them. 'He just likes to think of the old days. He *was* good when he was young. But he's old now. He forgets . . .' She laughed, but she didn't feel happy.

Caleb Tan was seventy years old. He had photographs of the Chinese Lion Dance all over the walls of his café. He was once a lion dancer himself. He danced with the best. He *was* the best. Everyone said so. Years ago, everybody wanted Quick Man Tan to dance the Lion Dance for them. It was their favourite dance and Caleb could dance it better than anybody else. At Chinese New Year he was everybody's favourite dancer. He danced under a big Chinese Lion's head made of paper. He moved his feet in a quick and beautiful way that everybody loved.

Then, after the dance, he did some fight moves. They looked like dances, too.

Caleb loved all the moves. But most of the fighting he did was in his head. He thought about fighting but he didn't often fight. He really could fight with his hands and feet. But he didn't fight very often. Only once or twice. That was enough for Caleb. He preferred to dance. He didn't really like fighting people. But he *did* like talking about it.

That was what he liked to do now – talk about the old

days. The café was his business but all Caleb wanted to do was talk. As he got older, his hearing got worse and his voice got louder.

Caleb talked to anybody who wanted to listen. Sometimes he talked when people didn't really want to listen. May May knew that most of the things he said were not true. But Caleb believed it all. It was more real to him than his business was. To Caleb, his café was just a place where he could tell stories. But May May knew they needed the café. It made them just enough money to live on.

Sometimes Caleb did a Lion Dance with children who were interested. He was slow, but you could see how good he once was. All the children liked to see the old man. He was something from the old days. There were not many like him around now.

*   *   *

Chinese New Year was always a busy time for everybody. It was one of the few times of the year when the café could do good business. May May worked more than ever at New Year. This year she really wanted Caleb to help her. She couldn't do everything. Sometimes people left the café after waiting too long for their food. All Caleb did was talk. People wanted their coffee and lunch, not his stories.

For Caleb, Chinese New Year was his favourite time. He had lots of people to listen to his stories. Sometimes other Lion Dancers came to the café. Then he shouted with happiness as he told them how to dance. And, of course, how he could dance better than anybody else.

'You see, my friends,' called out Caleb to a table full of bored tourists, 'it's all in the way you move. Like a circle,

6

like a wheel – like this . . .' And Caleb then turned round with his hands in front of him. His hands went right into May May and what she was carrying. The food was for a table full of tourists next to him. Everything fell to the floor. May May did her best to help the tourists but they left. Other people left, too. For once, Caleb was quiet and helped her.

May May was unhappy.

'It's not right!' May May told her husband that night. 'While you tell your stories I do all the work! There is too much for me and Henry to do.'

Henry was the cook. He was also their only son. He cooked everything. He was very good, but he had a lot to do in the kitchen. He needed someone to help him.

Henry dreamed of having the café to himself one day. He was already forty years old and still not married. There was no wife to help. There were no grandchildren to do little jobs. There was not enough money to pay for help.

Henry was a little like his father. He had his dreams. But he kept his dreams about the café to himself. In his head, he was always far away while he worked.

But now Henry was asleep. He couldn't hear his parents shouting. He couldn't hear Caleb tell May May to be quiet. He couldn't hear the hurt in his mother's voice. All Henry could hear was the sound of cooking in his dreams.

*   *   *

The words *Gong Xi Fa Chai* were written in red and yellow letters all over Singapore. This was Chinese for 'Happy New Year'. Sometimes old friends of Caleb and May May left *hong bao* in the café at this time. *Hong bao* are little red bags, usually with money inside. People always did this at Chinese New Year. Sometimes people left money, sometimes not. But they always left something. Poorer friends left oranges in place of money. Oranges are lucky. But May May was pleased when they got money. They always needed money. This year they got a lot of oranges.

Henry and May May wanted the café to do well this New Year. Henry worked very hard. He cooked more good food than he usually did. Lots of people came to the café. And Caleb couldn't talk to *all* of them. May May smiled a lot. She was busy but she was happy. Maybe business was getting better after all.

This time, Caleb *did* try to help. He brought coffee and food to the tables. He smiled as he worked. But then a young father with his children asked about the Lion Dance photographs on the walls. Caleb stopped what he was doing. He started to talk. May May heard him but she couldn't stop him. She was too busy. She wanted Caleb to get back to work before he did anything stupid.

It was early afternoon and there were lots of hungry people in the café. It was hot. But that didn't stop the rain. The rain started all at once. It came down and down on the roof of the café and made a loud, heavy sound. More people came in. They wanted to get out of the rain and have something to eat or drink. Caleb was happy. He could tell his stories while people stayed out of the rain. They could enjoy a good story while they ate their lunch. Why not? He thought it was good for business.

A young father and his two small children listened as Caleb talked. And talked. And talked. They were getting hungry. Caleb started to show them moves from the Lion

Dance. 'You turn, like a wheel – see?' Caleb told them in a loud voice. His hands moved in front of him. His feet moved, too. People were looking at him. Not all of them knew what he was doing. It just looked strange to them. And all the time the heavy rain fell.

By this time the café was full of people and all the tables were full. Some people were standing. They just wanted to be out of the rain. There wasn't much room for May May to do her work. People were talking and enjoying themselves while the rain fell outside.

Then a large young man pushed his way into the café. He was wearing a big jacket and he was very wet. His right hand was under his jacket and a bag was in his left hand. It was a travel bag – the kind tourists use to put passports and money in. The man looked afraid and he looked around him all the time. By mistake he pushed against a table. The man at the table was reading a magazine.

'Hey, watch where you're going!' said the man with the magazine in an angry voice. But the large young man brought his hand out from under his jacket. He had a dangerous-looking knife in it. He held the knife against the face of the man with the magazine.

'You just shut your mouth!' he shouted. 'See this knife! Don't start anything!'

9

As the young man spoke he turned around with the knife. He was talking to everybody in the café now. He sounded afraid. He looked dangerous. People put down their things and looked at him. They were all afraid. The café went quiet as the rain fell.

'Yes, feet too – just like a wheel!' said Caleb in a loud voice. He turned as he spoke and his foot moved quickly up into the air. His foot hit the big man's hand and the knife flew up into the air.

'Why, you stupid old man!' the young man shouted. Caleb smiled. He remembered his old fighting moves. In a minute the young man was on the floor. Somebody used a mobile phone to call the police. Soon they arrived and took the young man away in the rain.

A few minutes later the rain stopped.

*   *   *

The newspapers were full of the story the next day. 'Quick Man Tan' was once more in the news. The young man was a robber. The bag he had with him was a tourist's. That was why he ran to the café. He didn't want the police to find him.

'But he didn't know about "Quick Man Tan",' said the young father in the newspaper story. 'I saw it all with my two children. He just moved his foot in the air and then the knife flew away! He was just like Jackie Chan in the films! The children will never forget this. He was great!'

There were lots of *hong bao* for Caleb and May May after that. All of them had money inside. There was a lot of money this time.

With the money, May May found somebody to help

with the café. Her name was Elizabeth and she was a cook. Elizabeth and Henry worked very well together.

People asked Caleb to teach the Lion Dance to children. So that's what he did all the time now. He got paid for it, too. He didn't work at his café any more – he left that to Henry and May May. But he was happy.

Henry and Elizabeth got married a year later. The famous 'Quick Man Tan' did the Lion Dance on that day.

He wasn't quite so quick now. But nobody minded that.

'Turn like a wheel,' he laughed while he danced with the children. 'Like a wheel . . .'

The Wheel on the Wall

'Well, just take a look at that wheel!' Earl Cooper said to Candy, his wife. 'It must be much older than anything we have back home.'

When Earl Cooper travelled he always thought of home. But there weren't many really old buildings in Texas. Now he was in Portsmouth in the south of England. Portsmouth, Earl knew, was one of the best places to see old ships. Earl liked old things. They were staying at a pub which was very near to the sea. They could see lots of ships from the pub – that's why they liked it.

Earl was looking at the wall outside the pub. The pub's name, *The Old Swan*, was on the wall. Next to the name was a wooden ship's wheel and in the middle of the wheel was the name of a ship, *HMS Swan*. The wheel was old, Earl could tell. And it was there, just above his head.

The Old Swan was hundreds of years old. Earl knew because it said so on the sign by the wheel. It said that in the past sailors used the pub before they went to sea. Now the pub sold food and drink to tourists. They watched the ships and listened to the sea birds while they ate their meals.

Earl Cooper was sixty years old and both of his children – Marylou and Earl Junior – were parents themselves. Earl didn't work any more. He had enough money. More than enough.

Earl looked at the sign again. It told him how the oldest part of the pub was from 1350. The pub was bigger now, of course, but all of it was old. 'How can a place be so old?' thought Earl. And it was *still* being used.

'Are you getting ideas again, honey?' asked Candy. They always called each other 'honey'. 'You and your ideas! Sometimes you're just like a little boy, you big old thing!'

Candy liked to say things like that. But she liked him just as he was. Her husband loved finding out about the past.

Earl knew all about his family name of Cooper. The family came from Portsmouth – that was why they were on holiday there now. The last Cooper to live in Portsmouth was his great-grandfather, Benjamin Cooper. Benjamin sailed from Portsmouth in 1875 at the age of nineteen. He wanted to make himself rich in America. He didn't make himself rich but he had a good life. Benjamin died in Texas when he was sixty-three years old in 1919. It was just after the end of the First World War. Benjamin was waiting for his son, Ralph, to come back from the war in Europe. Just before Benjamin died, Ralph came back to America. He only had one arm now but he had a new wife. Ralph was Earl's grandfather.

Ralph Cooper always remembered the old things he saw in Europe in the war. He just loved stories about the past. He gave that love of the past to his children and to Earl. Earl was always his favourite grandson. Ralph told Earl lots of stories about old England. Other children heard cowboy stories from their grandfathers: Earl got old England.

Earl remembered Ralph. 'And here I am,' he thought to himself, 'standing in front of one of the oldest buildings I've ever seen. Not only that, it's in the very place where my great-grandfather, Benjamin Cooper, came from.'

Earl knew something else, too. Benjamin Cooper came to America on a sailing ship called *The Swan*. It was already an old ship in 1875 and Earl thought that there was nothing left of it now. But now he knew there *was* something left of the old ship. And there it was – the wheel on the wall of the *The Old Swan* pub.

Earl knew he wanted the wheel. He wanted to take it home to Texas. It was a part of his family history. It had to be his.

*   *   *

Earl and Candy had a good meal that evening, some fine English beer and then a good night's sleep. When he woke up, Earl knew just what to do. He told Candy all about it while they were eating breakfast.

'You know, honey, that ship's wheel is from old Benjamin Cooper's ship. I just know it. That's why I want to take it back home.'

'I understand, honey,' Candy answered with a smile. 'But it's part of this pub now.'

'I know!' said Earl with a loud laugh. 'But we can buy it! What do you think, Candy?'

Earl looked very happy and everyone in the room heard his laugh. People were looking at him.

'But honey,' asked Candy, 'what if they don't want to sell? What if they don't want anybody else to have their ship's wheel? After all, they've had it for all these years. It could be very expensive. They don't give things like that away for nothing, you know.'

'I've thought about that, honey,' Earl replied. 'And I agree with you. But everything has a price and I've got the money. Hey, they're a business, aren't they? They understand money all right, you just wait and see.'

After breakfast Earl asked to see Tony Thatcher. *The Old Swan* was Tony's pub. Tony was a small, thin man with a big smile. He wore nice clothes and was always friendly to the people who came to his pub. With rich tourists he was very friendly. His red Jaguar sports car was usually outside the pub. It was what they call a 'classic' car – it was old and cost a lot of money.

Tony Thatcher took Earl to his office while Candy had a coffee outside by the river. Earl said he could give Tony a lot of money for the ship's wheel. He told Tony about Benjamin Cooper and his family history. But Tony said no at first. After all, the wheel was very old and it was part of the pub's past.

'You can think of the past, Mr Thatcher – can I call you Tony? – or you can think of today. And with the money, Tony, you can buy another sports car. Maybe another old Jaguar? And, as I've told you, the wheel is part of my family's past, too. So you could say it's going back home, in a way. So, what do you say?'

*   *   *

A month later, Earl and Candy were smiling as they looked at the wall of their house in Houston, Texas. Earl thought to himself that, at last, he had a piece of his family's past. He was happy.

In Portsmouth, Tony Thatcher was happy, too. He was putting another Jaguar into his large garage. He was careful not to drive into any of the six ship's wheels in the garage. A friend of his made the wheels for him. They were just like the one that Earl bought. And there was another wheel on the outside wall of *The Old Swan* now. Old or new – Tony thought there was no way that a tourist could ever know which was which. Never in a hundred years.

Special Clay

Emilio Lopez was a boy with problems.

His family was poor and they didn't know what to do with him. He was thirteen years old, but his parents still couldn't find the right school for him. Not anywhere in Cleveland, Ohio in the USA. So far, not one of the schools wanted to have Emilio. They just couldn't help a boy with his 'difficulties'. That's what the schools all said.

Emilio was not a bad boy. He just got very angry sometimes. He got angry when he didn't understand things. He didn't like things that he couldn't understand. Not understanding something made him afraid and being afraid made him angry. He was a big boy for his age, too. His teachers didn't find it easy to stop him when he got angry. But he wasn't the kind of boy who liked to get into fights. No, he usually broke things or sent furniture flying across the room. But breaking things could be dangerous. He could hurt somebody – or himself – doing things like that.

His parents were very unhappy about their son. They wanted to do the best for him. But they knew that, one day, he could get into real difficulties. Then a doctor from a university came to see Emilio. He was somebody who knew all about the kind of problems Emilio had. He said Emilio needed special help.

The doctor said Emilio needed to go to a special school where there were young people like him. The students lived at the school. His parents were pleased to hear that the school was free. It was also good for them for Emilio to be away from home for a while. His father and mother loved Emilio, but they also had three other children to look after.

Emilio didn't say a lot but everybody knew he was intelligent. He found it difficult to make friends or talk to people. He wanted to talk – everybody knew that. But there was something that stopped him. It was like there was a wall there that was too high for him to get over. This wasn't easy for him, and sometimes not being able to say what he meant made him angry. That was the biggest problem.

Then there were other times when Emilio couldn't stop talking. But the things he talked about were things few people wanted to know about. When Emilio got interested in something, he talked about nothing else. And Emilio got interested in things like car numbers. Or railway trains. Or the names of all the players in his favourite baseball team for the last thirty years. This made it difficult for anybody to have a real conversation with Emilio. Most people got very bored after the first half hour. And when people got bored, Emilio got angry.

The special school was on the far side of Cleveland. It was a nice place and the teachers were kind, too. They taught all of the usual things at the school but the classes were a lot smaller. Things didn't look very different to Emilio – at first. And, at first, he was just the same as ever. After a while, he found he liked maths and science. But his favourite class was drama.

The teacher Emilio liked best was Mrs McFee, the drama teacher. She was small and round and she was sixty-three years old. She had white hair and a big smile. Emilio was tall and thin. He had black hair and a sad look on his face.

Emilio was a lot taller than Mrs McFee. Teacher and student couldn't be more different to look at.

But they liked each other at once.

Mrs McFee's drama classes let Emilio be himself. He could be angry if he wanted. It was OK. But that didn't happen very often now. Mrs McFee made everything into a game they could all play. Everybody knew what to do in her classes. Emilio liked that. He liked things he could easily understand. He also liked the games they played in the drama classes. His favourite game was one Mrs McFee called 'special clay'. In the school pottery classes Emilio used real clay to make things. But Mrs McFee's special clay was different.

'Right,' Mrs McFee told the students. 'Here is some special clay. Why is it so special? I'll tell you why: it's because you can make it into anything you like. It can be big; it can be small. It can be a car, a baseball bat – anything. But, most of all, you must see the thing in your head just as if it was in front of you. Then, in a very careful way, you make the thing with your hands. After that, you show us how to use it. Then, once you've finished, you just make the thing small again and put it back into your pocket.'

But Mrs McFee had no clay. There was nothing there. Her hands were empty. But nobody ever said so. It was all real to them at the time. Emilio believed it more than anybody. He was always most careful to make things just right. And when his car or his boat or his guitar was ready, it was just as if it was really there. And not just for Emilio – everybody else in the class believed it, too. Until the game was over. For those few minutes Emilio couldn't be happier.

Things got better for Emilio. Nobody said he could be just like everybody else. But, for the first time ever, Emilio felt he could do something with his life. To Emilio and everybody who knew him, that meant a lot.

Mrs McFee's drama classes also helped Emilio with his anger. Before then, his anger was like a wall in front of his mind. It was a problem he couldn't get over. But now, at last, his anger was a problem he could do something about.

Emilio's teachers soon found that he was very good at pottery. He could make things out of clay that were quite beautiful. He made little people and animals that looked just like the real thing. But you always knew they were made by Emilio. There was something about them that you couldn't mistake for anyone else's work.

By the time Emilio was nearly sixteen he was doing very well at school. He still had problems, but he was much better than before. He was also becoming well-known as a good young potter. People already wanted to buy the things he made. He could make quite a lot of money from pottery, everybody was sure. Mrs McFee knew Emilio could learn to be a great potter. All he needed was the right teacher. Mrs McFee wanted to make sure he got that teacher.

She had a friend who was a well-known potter. His name was Grover Jackson and he had a pottery studio which was next to Lake Erie. Grover was the best potter she knew – and a good teacher. He made the kind of things in clay that Emilio loved. Grover also liked to see good young potters work at his studio.

Mrs McFee and his parents took Emilio to see Grover. The boy and the potter liked each other right away. Grover said Emilio could be a fine potter. Emilio could work with him. He could learn from him and stay in a room at his studio. He said Emilio could sell anything he made and could make some money. This was good news for Emilio and his parents. Emilio, of course, loved the studio and couldn't wait to start work.

But first he had to go home and get his things ready.

Mrs McFee had a big green and white car. It was thirty years old and people often told her to get a new car. But she never did. She liked old things. She said she could take Emilio and his things to Grover's studio in her old car. There was lots of room in it. Emilio's parents liked Mrs McFee and were happy for her to help.

The day came, at last, when Emilio was ready to go. He knew how important this day was, not only to himself but to his family as well. And, of course, to his good friend Mrs McFee. Thanks to her, he wasn't just another boy with problems. That's what he thought. And he was probably right.

Emilio still had some problems of course. Talking to people still wasn't easy for him, but he could look after himself now. He could cook and clean, and knew how to drive a car.

It was still early in the morning when Mrs McFee's old green and white car arrived. Emilio and his family were already waiting outside. His family were all feeling both sad and happy, at the same time. Emilio felt the same way – he was sad to leave but happy to go. Emilio put his few things into the car. After saying goodbye to his family, Emilio and Mrs McFee were off.

The pottery studio was about an hour's drive away from Emilio's home. Everything was fine. Mrs McFee was a careful driver and the day was warm. Soon they could see the blue waters of Lake Erie through the open windows of the car. But, after a while, the waters of the lake began to turn grey. The sky became dark. It began to rain. Mrs McFee turned her car into the road that led to Grover's studio. She knew they were now only a few kilometres away.

The rain didn't stop. It got worse. They closed all the car windows. Soon the heavy rain made it very difficult to see the road. Mrs McFee slowed down as she looked for a good place to stop the old car. But the young man in the fast sports car behind her didn't slow down until it was too late. The sports car hit the back of Mrs McFee's car. Both cars then came to a stop at the side of the road.

Emilio was lucky. His seat-belt kept him safe. He looked at Mrs McFee. She was still wearing her seat-belt but her eyes were closed. Emilio didn't know what to do. At first he felt angry like he did when he was at school. How could something this bad happen? Why now? But he knew he mustn't get angry. He *must* do something – but what?

He got out of Mrs McFee's car and looked at the sports car. He saw that the driver was not much older than him.

There was blood on the driver's face and his eyes were closed. Emilio knew he must get help. Mrs McFee didn't have a mobile phone. She didn't like them. Did the young man have a phone with him? He looked. Yes! There was a phone on the floor of the sports car. But it was broken.

At first, Emilio thought of waiting for another car to come and stopping it. But the road was quiet and not many cars used it. It could be a long time before a car came and he didn't have time. No, he must do something himself. The rain stopped. Emilio thought hard. Perhaps *he* could drive one of the cars.

The sports car was no good, but Mrs McFee's car looked OK. Maybe he could take the young man and Mrs McFee to the pottery studio in it. Grover Jackson could get help for them then.

Emilio looked carefully at Mrs McFee's car. One of the back tyres was no good. The other tyres looked OK. He didn't know how badly hurt the sports car driver and Mrs McFee were. He must get them to Grover's studio. But how? He needed one more wheel but there wasn't one. He felt his anger again.

Then Mrs McFee's voice spoke to him inside his head.

'You must see it in your head, just like it was in front of you. Then, in a very careful way, you make it with your hands . . .'

Of course! All his anger was gone. He *knew* what to do.

*　　*　　*

When Grover Jackson saw young Emilio Lopez driving Mrs McFee's car up to the pottery studio, he knew something was wrong. He called for help right away.

Fifteen minutes later, Grover and Emilio were talking to two policemen. Mrs McFee was getting into an ambulance. The young man from the sports car was all right – thanks to Emilio. The police all said that Emilio was a fine young man. Emilio was trying to tell them what happened. They were asking him a lot of questions.

One of the policemen said that you could not drive Mrs McFee's car with only three wheels. But Grover was sure he saw four wheels on the car when it arrived. The policeman said, 'I'm sorry, sir, but there are only three wheels on the car.'

But Grover just knew he saw four wheels on the car. Yet, when he looked again, he saw only three wheels. Why was that? What happened? Could Emilio tell him where the fourth wheel came from? Where was it now?

'Hey!' Mrs McFee shouted from the ambulance. She was fine, but she wasn't going anywhere without seeing Emilio first. She told the police that the hospital could wait a little longer for her.

Emilio wasn't the kind of boy to put his arms around people he liked. He just gave a big smile when he saw her. The smile told Mrs McFee all she needed to know. Grover put his arms around her and laughed.

Grover told Mrs McFee about the fourth wheel. She looked very interested but said nothing. Then Grover asked Emilio about the wheel.

Emilio answered by putting his hand on his pocket.

Emilio knew the car needed another wheel. Then he remembered Mrs McFee's drama classes:

'*You must see it in your head just like it was in front of you. Then, in a very careful way, you make it with your hands.*'

All it needed was for him to believe. So he made the wheel. And he *did* believe in it. And it *did* work, just like she told him. And, when the job was finished, he put it back into his pocket.

So Emilio spoke just two words to answer Grover.

Grover Jackson thought he knew a lot about clay. But he didn't understand the answer Emilio gave.

Emilio knew. He and Mrs McFee knew. They both laughed as they said the words again together – *special clay*.

The Trishaw Man

Gregory Lim was only thirteen years old, but he was the best student in his class. All his teachers said he was doing very well. 'Singapore needs young people like him,' they said. 'He'll go far.'

But Gregory wasn't very good at sport. He wasn't bad but he wasn't good. It wasn't important. Not really. He was intelligent but he wasn't strong.

Gregory's father, Thomas Lim, was strong, very strong, and he loved his son. No father could feel better about his son than Thomas did. He was always thinking about his only child. Thomas drove a trishaw and he worked for many hours a day. He drove people around on a three-wheeled trishaw bicycle. The bicycle pulled a seat for two people. It had a kind of big umbrella at the back. This went over the seat to keep the sun out of people's eyes. Thomas often had two or sometimes three people in his trishaw. They sat under the umbrella while he pulled them around in the hot sun.

Sometimes taxi drivers got angry with him because the trishaw was slow. The taxi drivers also didn't like Thomas taking business away from them. But that didn't happen so often now. Years ago people used trishaws a lot. But people these days usually wanted taxis because they were quicker. Trishaws were too slow for most people. Only tourists on holiday used them. And, sometimes, old people who liked to remember the old days. Thomas often had to work well into the night to make enough money to live on.

Gregory's mother, Anita, liked to think of her son as she worked at a fish shop. Every time she cleaned a fish or put a kilo of prawns in a bag she thought of her only child. She didn't mind all the hard work and the smell of the fish on her skin. It was all done for her son. The money from Anita's job at the fish shop helped to pay for Gregory's school things.

Yes, it was a hard life for Thomas and Anita, and everything they did was for their son. Gregory was going to get a good job and look after them when they were old.

Gregory went to school by bus. He hated it when other students arrived at school in taxis or cars. The rich students came in their fathers' new Mercedes or comfortable taxis. He was the best student but it was the others who had money. That's how Gregory saw it. They were the ones with nice new clothes. They played computer games. They ate hamburgers at expensive fast food restaurants when they wanted to.

And everybody knew his parents were poor. That's what

Gregory hated most. They all knew his father drove a trishaw. Everybody saw his father pulling tourists around in the hot sun. Could there ever be a worse job than that? Why, driving an old taxi was better than driving a trishaw!

Gregory wasn't the only one from a poor family. Many other students also had two working parents. But their fathers had better jobs than his father. *They* didn't work in the hot sun and they wore nice clothes. *They* got paid every month.

Gregory loved his father. He knew how hard he worked. If only his father had a different job. Gregory was an 'A' student! But his father was a poor trishaw driver. It was all wrong.

No, Gregory never forgot what his father did. But he often wanted to.

*   *   *

'Ayuh!' said Thomas to himself as he pulled the trishaw up a hill. There were two heavy tourists in the back and the roads were full today. It was National Day – a holiday in Singapore. It was very busy and everybody was having a party. People were out in the streets. The red and white colours of Singapore were everywhere. It was a good time for business for Thomas. Cars were slow on the busy roads. This was one of the few times that Thomas's trishaw could be quicker than a car. It was a good time to make money but it was hard work. After all, he wasn't getting any younger.

His two tourists wanted to see the famous Raffles Hotel. It was a favourite place for tourists. On that day there was another visitor to the hotel – a beautiful and very famous film star called Dianne Troy. She was making a film in

Singapore. Dianne was having a day off from filming and wanted to rest. But she had lots of fans who wanted to see her. Everybody knew Dianne Troy was staying at Raffles.

The street outside the hotel was very busy. People were there for National Day and also to see their favourite film star. There were hundreds of people all around the front of the hotel. They all wanted to see Dianne Troy. The fans were happy but after a time they felt uncomfortable. The sun was hot and it wasn't easy for people to move. There were just too many people there. All the taxis coming to the hotel moved slowly because of the crowd. It was still early in the afternoon. The day was at its hottest.

Thomas could get to the hotel quite quickly. He knew his way around Singapore better than almost anybody. He knew all the shortest ways that cars were too big to use. And it was easier for a trishaw to move through lots of people. Cars were much slower. Thomas always called out in a loud voice to let people know he was coming.

The trishaw stopped outside Raffles Hotel and the two tourists got out. They wanted to see Dianne Troy too. There were cameras everywhere. And so many people! The two tourists took out their cameras and Thomas said goodbye. He was about to go when Dianne Troy came to the window. Everybody pushed to the front to get a better look. All the people were very close together. Dianne Troy smiled and waved to the fans and they shouted back.

Then Thomas saw something at the front of the crowd. A woman was calling loudly for help. But why? Then he saw why. The woman was trying to stop a young girl from falling. It wasn't easy with all those people around them.

The girl was about twelve years old. Both the woman and the girl looked like tourists.

'My daughter!' the woman shouted. 'A hornet stung her! Please help me. She needs a doctor quickly!' There were shouts from the people around her. They all knew that hornets in Singapore are very dangerous.

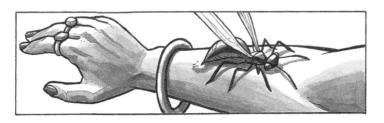

Hornets can kill children or old people. Everybody is afraid when they see the big black and yellow insects.

But the nearest hospital was far away. The woman couldn't walk through the streets carrying the sick child. Certainly not when the streets were as busy as this. A taxi was too slow in these crowds. But Thomas knew what to do.

*   *   *

Gregory Lim felt very pleased. He was looking at a page from *The Straits Times*, Singapore's biggest newspaper. Lots of students were looking at it. The page was up on the school wall.

Tourist Stung By Hornet – Film Star Says 'Thank You' to Trishaw Driver

Thomas Lim, a Singapore trishaw driver, took a very sick Australian girl to hospital yesterday. A hornet stung the girl, twelve-year-old Tracey Kinsella from Melbourne, on the arm outside Raffles Hotel. "I was so afraid for Tracey," her mother, Mrs Lauren Kinsella, said. "Insect stings make her very ill. She had to see a doctor at once."

Police Officer Melvin Yip, who was at the hotel, told this newspaper what happened. "The crowds of people made things worse for Miss Kinsella. The girl needed help quickly. A taxi couldn't get through the crowded streets in time. It certainly was quick thinking from Mr Lim. With his trishaw he was much faster than any car. Yes, Miss Kinsella is well now because of Mr Lim, I'm sure of that."

Miss Dianne Troy, the famous film star, saw what happened. "I saw it all from my hotel window," Miss Troy told this newspaper. "I was saying hello to my lovely Singapore fans at the time. Then I saw that poor girl. She looked very sick but Mr Lim was so good. He knew just what to do, and got that poor girl to a doctor in time."

Gregory smiled as the students read the newspaper story on the wall. That was his father they were reading about.

His father, the trishaw driver.

Beautiful Thing

'Beautiful! Very, very beautiful! Where did you find it?' the professor asked.

'Well,' I said. 'I didn't really find it – it found me.'

Professor Selkirk looked very happy and I was feeling happy myself.

'I've been at university for two years now,' I thought, 'and this is the first time he has said something nice to me.' OK – I know all the other students have found interesting things. But not me. *I* never found anything. Not until now. Now I was, at last, someone he was interested in.

The professor smiled at me. He had quite a nice face really. Old but kind.

'You have to be a real archaeologist to find something like this, Polly,' the professor said.

'*Polly!* He usually calls me "Miss Hopkins". He must really like what I've found,' I thought to myself.

'Yes,' he went on. 'A *real* archaeologist sees right away what something is. That's what we're here for. We're here to study things from the past; things we find in the earth. We can learn important things – if we know how to look. So, how did this beautiful thing find *you?*'

I looked again at the beautiful thing he had in his hands. It was round and as big as my hand. It looked like a little wheel from something. A thin, silver-coloured wheel. It was dirty but you could still see its lovely silver colour. Like a CD. But there were lines on it. Was it writing of some sort? Maybe.

'It was strange,' I said. 'I mean, I wasn't looking for anything unusual. Then, all at once, it was there at my feet. I know that sounds stupid but that's how it happened, really.'

'That's OK, Polly. We archaeologists know what that means, don't we?' the professor said.

My face told him that I didn't know.

'It's what we call "the nose". He laughed. '"The nose" is the feeling you get when you know something is important.

It doesn't look important at first but it is. That's when you *really* know archaeology, when you can do that. It's really wonderful.'

It was nice that the professor thought I had "the nose". But I knew I didn't. No, the silver disc really did come from nowhere. It was just like it decided to find me. But I couldn't say that to the professor now. Not when he'd just said I had "the nose".

'So, er, what do you think it is, Professor Selkirk?' I asked.

'You know, Polly,' he replied with a smile, 'I have no idea.'

I couldn't believe what I was hearing. I mean, I always thought the professor knew everything. Why didn't he say it was Roman or something? After all, he's the professor of archaeology here, not me.

'Er, is it Roman or something?' I asked. I was trying to help.

'Well, Polly, I've never seen anything like it before. I think I'll have to ask some people to take a look at it. You know, this really is very, very beautiful!'

So, no Romans, then. 'What about the lines on it?' I asked. 'Is it some kind of writing?'

'Maybe,' he said. 'I'm afraid I just don't know. All I know is that it's old. It has to be.'

'How do you know it's old?' I asked again – it was unusual for me to ask so many questions. 'Maybe it's some kind of CD or something.'

'Then they were making CDs about two thousand years ago,' he answered in a quiet voice. 'You see the earth around it, Polly? Look at the colour. This disc hasn't seen the light of day for hundreds – thousands – of years. Anybody can see that. This thing is older than it looks. And anyway, there's no hole in the centre. And CDs all have a hole in the centre, don't they?'

*   *   *

The professor asked some people to come to the university and look at the disc. They were at the university for a week. I don't know what they did to the disc, but it wasn't long before they asked me to speak to them. They wanted to ask me lots of questions. I was, after all, the person who found the disc.

Professor Selkirk was in his office with two people – a man and a woman. They were older than the professor and looked important.

'Dr Janet Collins and Dr Danny Fellows are old friends of mine,' the professor said. 'They know more about the archaeology of early Britain than anybody in the world. They want to ask you a few questions, Polly. Is that OK?'

They asked questions all right. They asked questions all afternoon. And not only about the disc. Three hours of questioning later, they knew more about me than I did! They were very nice about it and they never made me feel uncomfortable. But by the time they finished, my life was like an open book to them.

Were they *really* just archaeologists?

'Do you mind if we take some DNA from the inside of your mouth?' asked Dr Collins in a friendly voice. 'It won't hurt.'

DNA? It's everywhere in our bodies. It's what makes each

of us different. They can find DNA in just one hair, and everybody has different DNA.

'Of course not,' I said. I was sure there were things that they weren't telling me. Still, I did as they asked. Why not?

'It's OK, Polly,' said Professor Selkirk. 'They asked for my DNA too. They want DNA from all the people who have had the disc in their hands.'

'So where is the disc?' I asked. 'I'd like to see it again.'

'Oh, you will, Polly,' said the professor. 'But we want to look at it for a little longer first.'

'How long?'

'Just a day or two – no time at all,' Dr Fellows replied with a smile. 'Then we'll talk again.'

*   *   *

I just couldn't sleep. All I could do was think about the disc. What was it? Why did it mean so much to me? I knew it was unusual for a student to find something important. But there was more to it than that. I knew that, in some way, the disc wanted me. Like it was calling out to me. I know it sounds stupid. After all, how can something thousands of years old speak to you?

I didn't do much studying. I tried but I couldn't do it. All I thought about was the disc. About how beautiful and strange it was. I didn't really think it was Roman. I didn't think that anybody knew anything about it. That's why the professor's friends asked me so many questions – because they didn't know much themselves. I was sure of that.

Three days later I was having breakfast in the university café, as usual. It was only half past eight in the morning.

37

There were still thirty minutes to go before my first class – it was about Roman buildings. I usually have breakfast with other students and talk to them. Today I chose to eat alone and read a book about the Romans. I was just getting to one of the more interesting bits when there was a hand on my shoulder. At first I thought it was one of my friends.

'Sorry – can't talk – I'm reading,' I said, not looking up from my book.

'It's nice to see you working so hard, Miss Hopkins,' said a voice I knew. But it wasn't another student. It was Dr Fellows. Dr Collins was with him. They both laughed.

'But today you can stop for a little,' said Dr Collins. 'We have some important things to talk about. But not here. Let's go to the professor's office.'

*　　*　　*

Professor Selkirk's office wasn't very big and it looked a little strange. It was quite a new office with computers and other new things. But everywhere you looked there were things from the past next to them. And there was the professor sitting at his desk. The disc was on the desk in front of him. He smiled. But the look in his eyes told me he had something important to say. I felt hot in that small room with three other people.

'Polly, please sit down.'

We all sat down: me in front of the professor's desk and the others behind it. I felt like a little girl at school again. I waited for somebody to speak.

'You said the disc looked like a CD,' the professor began. 'Dr Collins thinks that perhaps you are right, Polly.'

I didn't say anything but my mouth opened. I closed it quickly.

'You see,' Dr Collins said. 'We didn't understand what the lines on the disc were at first. We looked at the disc in all kinds of ways. We looked at the earth from the disc. But we found nothing.'

'Then last night the disc was on a desk next to a computer,' said Dr Fellows. 'When we turned the computer on something very strange happened. The lines on the disc changed. We all saw it. It was almost like the disc knew about computers. Like it wanted to speak to us.'

'So . . . what did the disc say?' I asked.

'See for yourself,' replied the professor.

He gave me the disc and I looked at it carefully. The lines were now a picture of something. I knew what it was. I remembered it from school. It was a picture of DNA.

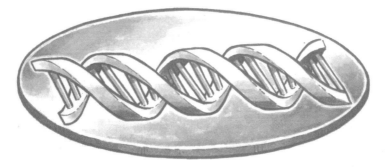

'I can see you know what it is,' Dr Fellows smiled. 'But this DNA – the one in the picture – is rather different. It isn't from the professor or from us. It isn't from anybody else at the university. Except you. You see, Polly, this is a picture of *your* DNA.'

'And what's more . . .' Dr Collins began.

But the professor spoke before Dr Collins could finish. 'Perhaps this isn't the right time. Polly has heard enough for now, don't you think?'

'No, Professor. We have to tell her,' Dr Collins answered. 'And now is a good time to do it.'

I didn't like the sound of this. Tell me what?

Dr Fellows spoke now. 'You see, Polly, the DNA in the picture is *yours*. There's no mistake about that. But there's something else . . .'

'And what's that?' I asked.

'The DNA in the picture – *your* DNA – isn't from a person. It's different,' Dr Fellows said slowly. 'It looks like a person's DNA, but it isn't. We haven't ever seen anything like it before. Not anywhere on Earth.'

'What are you saying?' I shouted. 'My family are from London! Now you tell me that we're from Mars or something! Don't be stupid!'

'We're not saying anything more for now,' said Dr Collins. 'Maybe the disc changed your DNA. Maybe not. We don't know. But we need you to stay with us. That's the only way we'll find an answer.'

'Stay with you?' I asked. 'What do you mean? Where? For how long? I mean, I have work to do!'

'It's all right, Polly,' said the professor. 'I've already spoken to the university. You can have all the time you need. They understand.'

'Do they?' I answered. I was feeling rather angry with them. 'I'm not sure I do. Are you saying I can't go home until you find answers to all this? Do I have to stay here until you can read an old CD?'

Of course, I didn't really think of the disc like that. But I like going home to my flat and I like going out with my friends. I don't like being told what to do or where to go. Who were they to stop me from doing these things?

'That's just what we *are* saying,' said Dr Collins. I didn't like the way she said it. Her voice wasn't so friendly any more. 'And the disc is something we don't understand yet. It could be something we've never seen before.'

'It's not my problem,' I shouted as I got up from my chair. 'I'm me – a student. I'm not from Mars! I'm going home now and nobody is going to stop me.'

And nobody tried to stop me. Not until I opened the door and found two large men there. 'Excuse me,' I said. I tried to get past them. It was like trying to walk through a wall.

I looked back at the professor. His face looked sad. Perhaps he couldn't do anything about any of this. I didn't know.

'So, you really do mean it?' I asked, looking at the two doctors. They said nothing. 'You know, I don't think you two are just archaeologists. You're not, are you?'

'We are,' said Dr Fellows. 'But we do other important things too. Now I think it's best if you come along with us.'

I'm not usually the kind of person who gets angry easily. But this time I couldn't stop myself. I went over to the table and took the disc in my hands. I did it before anybody had time to stop me.

'It's all because of this little thing,' I told them, 'so I'm taking it.'

They all stood up. They all told me to be careful – that there was no need to be angry. I wasn't listening to them.

'I'm going to walk out of that door. Try to stop me and I'll break this stupid disc in two!'

I didn't really know how to break it. But they didn't want me to try. The two large men at the door also looked very uncomfortable.

Then the strangest thing happened. The disc in my hand sent out strong light, like a little sun. I couldn't look at it, but it wasn't hot. I closed my eyes. A second later I opened my eyes again and looked at my hand.

My hand was empty. The disc was gone.

*   *   *

The next week they let me go back to my studies. The strange thing was, they couldn't find anything different about my DNA any more. They couldn't understand it. They looked at my DNA many more times, but now there was nothing unusual about it. After a while they said it was all a mistake. Anyway, they let me get back to my flat and my friends.

And the disc? They said it wasn't really old or unusual after all. Really, the disc was nothing more than a CD. It was a mistake and they were sorry. But it was best for me not to tell anyone. Anyone at all. Didn't I think that was best? Maybe I did.

I never said anything about the disc to Professor Selkirk again. I didn't really know what to say to him.

But I knew the disc was real. Was it from some other world? Was another world trying to say something to us? I was sure of it. Maybe the disc saw how angry I was. Perhaps it knew this was not the right time to talk to us. Yes, there was a mistake. But was it *our* mistake or not?

You tell me.

Cambridge English Readers

Look out for other titles in the series:

Level 2

Jojo's Story
by Antoinette Moses

'There aren't any more days. There's just
time. Time when it's dark and time when
it's light. Everything is dead, so why not
days too?'

Everyone in Jojo's village is dead, and
ten-year-old Jojo is alone.

Different Worlds
by Margaret Johnson

'In my world, there are no birds singing.
No babies crying.'

Sam is like any other teenage girl except
that she was born deaf. Now she loves Jim,
but are their worlds too different?

Double Bass Mystery
by Jeremy Harmer

Penny Wade is a musician. She is in
Barcelona with her orchestra. But her
double bass is lost, and then someone with
her orchestra dies. The police want to
know what happened, and Penny's life
changes as she learns the truth.

Within High Fences
by Penny Hancock

'There was nothing different about that
night. But my life was changing.'

It's the night when Nancy meets
George. But there's Nancy's job and her
boyfriend. And will George have to return
to his own country?

44

Superbird
by Brian Tomlinson

A spaceship crashes on a strange planet and everyone on it dies – except for Mary Mount. She helps the people of the planet to build their own spaceship and then returns home in it. But when she is back home, the trouble really begins.

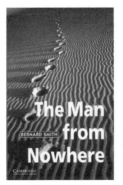

The Man from Nowhere
by Bernard Smith

A man is walking slowly in the desert. He is not wearing a shirt. The sun is on his back, which is burnt red. He cannot see, he cannot think. He does not know where he is or who he is. He only knows that he must keep moving. Keep moving, or die.

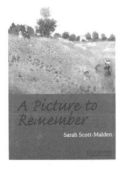

A Picture to Remember
by Sarah Scott-Malden

Cristina Rinaldi works for an art museum in Buenos Aires. One day she has a motorbike accident and can't remember some things. But there are two men who think she remembers too much, and they want to kill her before she tells the police what she saw.

Logan's Choice
by Richard MacAndrew

'I'm Inspector Logan of the Edinburgh police,' Jenny said. 'I'm very sorry about the death of your husband.'

Who killed Alex Maclennan? His friend, his wife or her brother? It isn't easy, but Logan has to choose.

Level 3

The House by the Sea
by Patricia Aspinall

Carl and Linda Anderson buy a weekend house by the sea. But one weekend Linda does not arrive at the house, and Carl begins to worry. What has happened to her?

Just Good Friends
by Penny Hancock

It's Stephany and Max's first holiday away together. They go to Italy and stay at Stephany's friend Carlo's flat in a Mediterranean village. But Carlo's wife is not very happy to see Stephany – and the two couples find out why, and a lot of other things about each other, in a hot Italian summer.

The Ironing Man
by Colin Campbell

While Tom is at work in London, his wife Marina is left bored at home. She wishes for someone to do the housework for her and the Ironing Man enters her life. Soon everything begins to change for Marina and Tom.

Double Cross
by Philip Prowse

Secret agent Monika Lundgren chases a would-be killer, and meets a mysterious football team, a rock musician, and a madman with dreams of world power . . .

The Lahti File
by Richard MacAndrew

'Foreign executive' Ian Munto is sent to
Lahti in Finland to investigate some
strange events. When a man is killed in
front of him, Munro starts looking for
answers and discovers a poisonous secret.

Eye of the Storm
by Mandy Loader

In Florida, a man is out fishing in the sea,
not knowing that a hurricane is coming.
His daughter Ikemi and her boyfriend
Max must try to save him.

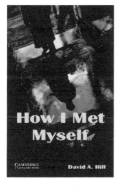

How I Met Myself
by David A. Hill

In a dark street in Budapest, John Taylor
meets someone who changes his life. But
who is this man? And what is he trying to
tell John?

The Beast
by Caroline Walker

'You may see something moving in the
corner of your eye. If you turn to look,
there will be nothing there.'

In Wales, Susie meets the 'undead'. Is it
a man, or an animal?

Cambridge English Readers

Other short stories in this series by Frank Brennan:

Level 3

Tales of the Supernatural

Six stories about a world we cannot explain – a film star discovers the dangers of dancing with a stranger, a man comes face to face with his father's past, an Irish-American family cannot escape someone from the past, a woman doesn't listen when she is told not to destroy a very old tree, an English writer slowly becomes more and more Japanese, and a killer 'sees' himself die in hospital.

Level 5

Windows of the Mind

Each of these highly entertaining stories is about one of the five senses. We meet a well-known broadcaster whose blindness is her power, a war hero who hates noise and wants silence, a wine-taster who has an accident, a university lecturer who learns Tai Chi, and a magazine journalist who smells scandal and will do anything for a good story.

Level 4

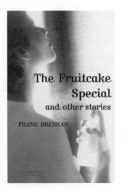

The Fruitcake Special and other stories

Five stories about discovery – a perfume that attracts men, a book that shows people's thoughts, a remarkable change in a widow's life, the secret of high intelligence, and a way of making time stand still – make up this entertaining collection.